A WORLD OF GODS

ROAR!

I0795533

HINDU
Gods

by Eliza Nodes

BEARPORT PUBLISHING

Roar! Books, an imprint of Bearport Publishing by FlutterBee

Credits
All images are courtesy of Shutterstock.com, unless otherwise stated. Recurring – C_Atta, Macrovector, Anna Timoshenko; Cover, © Dmitry Rukhlenko_Madhya, R.M. Nunes; 4–5, © fireFX, prudhvichowdary, CC BY 4.0 < https://creativecommons.org/licenses/by/4.0/> via Wikimedia Commons; 6, © AstroVed.com; 7, © mrinalpal; 8–9, © Yuriy Mazur, public domain via Wikimedia Commons; 10–11, © Thunot Duvotenay (1796-1875), Public domain, via Wikimedia Commons; 12–13, © Alexandra Lande, public domain via Wikimedia Commons; 14–15, © steve estvanik; 16–17, © thala bhula, tinka's; 18–19, © Deepk Creation; 20–21, © SNEHIT PHOTO, Wirestock Creators; 22–23, © Itiprithul, godongphoto; 24–25, © public domain via Wikimedia Commons, CC0 BY 1.0 < https://creativecommons.org/publicdomain/zero/1.0/> via Wikimedia Commons; 28–29, © public domain via Wikimedia Commons, CC0 BY 1.0 < https://creativecommons.org/publicdomain/zero/1.0/> via Wikimedia Commons; 30–31, © Vivek BR, Point designz.

Bearport Publishing Company Product Development Team
Kayla Eggert, Theresa Emminizer, Kim Jones, Allison Juda, Naomi Reich, Steve Scheluchin, Tiana Tran

Library of Congress Cataloging-in-Publication Data is available at www.loc.gov or upon request from the publisher.

ISBN: 979-8-89577-853-1 (hardcover)
ISBN: 979-8-89577-857-9 (paperback)
ISBN: 979-8-89577-861-6 (ebook)

For more information, write to Bearport Publishing, 3500 American Blvd W, Suite 150, Bloomington, MN 55431. Printed in the United States of America.

CONTENTS

THE HINDU GODS

Hinduism is one of the world's oldest religions. The first record of it is from 1500 **BCE**. Today, there are more than a billion Hindus around the globe.

The oldest writings of Hinduism are the Vedas. This set of religious texts contains songs, prayers, and stories about the world and the Hindu gods.

Hinduism has one main god, named Brahman. However, different parts of Brahman are shown in thousands of other gods and goddesses. Six of these are split into two groups.

The Trimurti is a group of three gods. The Tridevi is a group of three goddesses.

THE TRIUMURTI

THE TRIDEVI

BRAHMA

Brahma is the god of creation. He is one of the gods in the Trimurti. Hindus believe Brahma created the world and everything in it.

Brahma is usually shown with four faces. Each face looks in a different direction. This represents the four texts that make up the Vedas. It also represents other ideas, such as the four directions.

In addition to four heads, Brahma has four arms. Each hand holds an item that is a symbol of his power. The flower shows his **divinity**, and the water pot is a symbol of creating life. The Vedas represent Brahma's wisdom, and the prayer beads are a symbol of time.

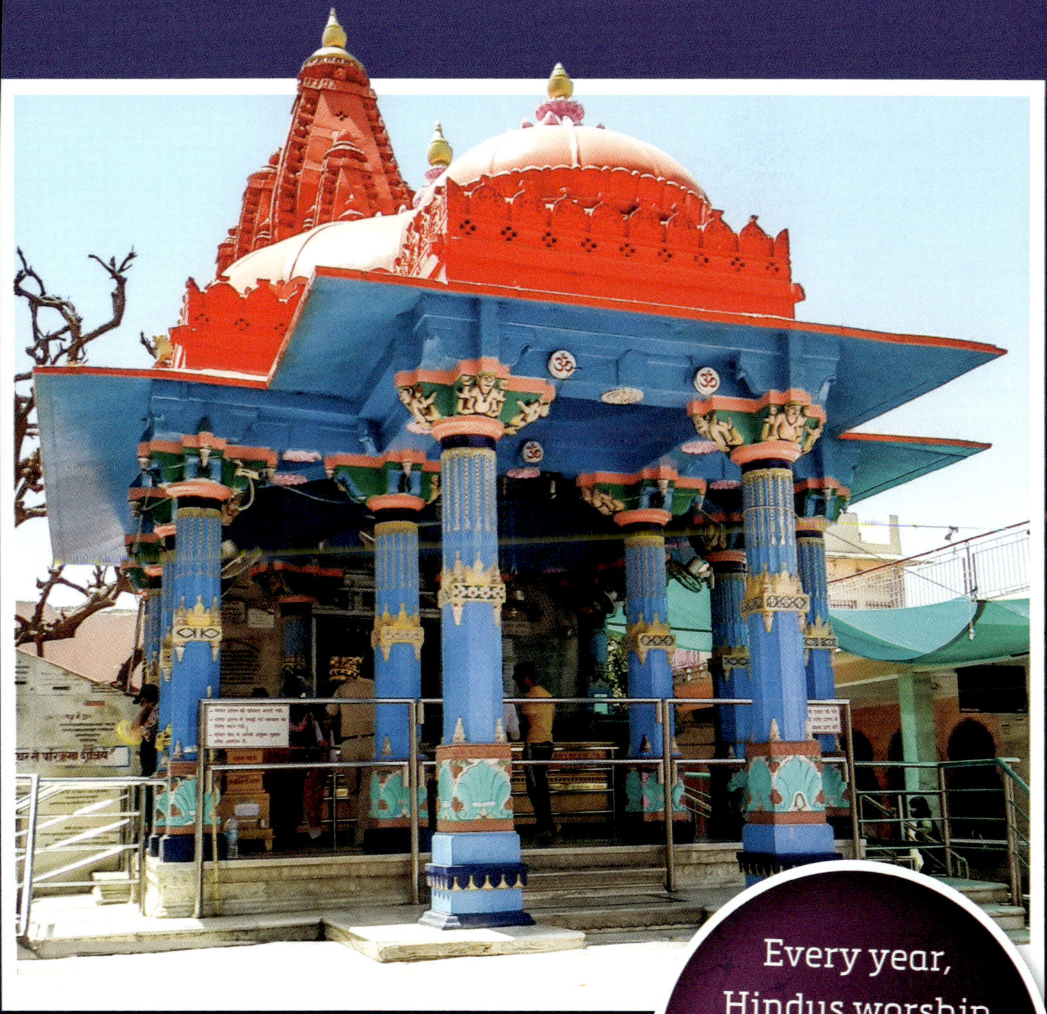

Every year, Hindus worship Brahma at his temple in Pushkar, India.

BRAHMA THE CREATOR

The Hindu story of creation begins with a golden egg. After hatching from the egg, Brahma made the world and everything in it.

As Brahma created things, he had to leave his body four times. First, he made **demons**. Brahma wanted to get away from their darkness. So, he left his body. This body became the night.

Next, Brahma made other gods. He also left this body, and it became the day. Then, Brahma made the **ancestors** and this body became **dusk**. Finally, Brahma made people and his body became dawn.

Brahma went on to create all other living things in the world. These included animals and plants.

VISHNU

Vishnu is another god within the Trimurti. He is the god of protection.

Vishnu is usually shown with blue skin. Like Brahma, he has four arms with each hand holding a symbol of power. Vishnu holds a lotus flower, a conch shell, and two weapons called a discus and a mace.

Hindus believe Vishnu lives on Mount Meru in a separate **realm** from Earth. This realm is called Vaikuntha. It is said to have beautiful gardens and be filled with sparkling gold and jewels.

Hindus believe that Vishnu comes back to Earth to fight against evil. He returns as 10 different **avatars**. He appears in one of these forms to restore good to the world.

THE THREE STEPS

The most famous Vishnu story is the **Legend** of the Three Steps. The gods were fighting with giants for control of the world. The gods asked Vishnu for help.

Vishnu turned into his smallest avatar and made an offer to the giants. He said the gods would own only as much of the world as he could cover in three steps.

Vishnu said the rest of the world would belong to the giants. The giants looked at Vishnu's short legs and agreed. They did not believe he could travel far!

Vishnu then became huge. In three steps, the new avatar covered the land, the sky, and the heavens. Nothing was left for the giants!

SHIVA

Shiva is the third member of the Trimurti. He is the god of destruction.

Shiva has a third eye on his forehead. This powerful eye can destroy things. Sometimes, he is shown with a cobra around his neck. Other times, he is wearing a necklace made of skulls.

Shiva is sometimes shown dancing. In this pose, one of his hands points at his left foot. This is a sign of saving people.

Like the other gods in the Trimurti, Shiva is often shown with four arms.

Shiva is married to the goddess Parvati. They have a son named Ganesh. Ganesh is a god made out of earth and clay.

THE ELEPHANT GOD

Parvati created Ganesh while Shiva was away. When Shiva returned, Parvati was busy bathing. Ganesh was guarding the door for her.

Shiva demanded to know who Ganesh was. Ganesh said that he was Parvati's son. Shiva became very angry.

Ganesh's head was chopped off as a punishment. Parvati opened the door and screamed when she saw what had happened. Then, Shiva realized he had made a terrible mistake.

Shiva sent servants to find a new head for his son. The first head they could find was from an elephant. Shiva attached the head to Ganesh's body, and the god lived again.

SARASWATI

Saraswati is one of the goddesses of the Tridevi. She is the goddess of knowledge and the arts. Each Tridevi goddess is married to a Trimurti god. Saraswati is Brahma's wife.

Saraswati often appears as a young woman. She is sometimes seen wearing a white **sari** to show her good nature.

Sometimes, Saraswati is shown riding a swan or peacock while playing a musical instrument. These are common symbols of the goddess.

Hindus pray to Saraswati for help with exams or musical skills. The goddess is worshipped during a festival at the start of spring. Her worshippers wear yellow, the color of wisdom.

SARASWATI'S CURSE

Although Saraswati was married to Brahma, one time she **cursed** him! One day, Brahma and the other gods were waiting for Saraswati. They could not begin an important ceremony without Brahma's wife.

The gods wanted to start the ceremony on time. Brahma asked the other gods what he should do. They decided to create a new wife for Brahma!

Brahma's new wife was called Gayatri. The gods could now begin the ceremony.

When Saraswati finally arrived, she was angry to see Brahma with a new wife. Saraswati cursed her husband to cause him to not to be worshipped by humans. Some say this is why there are not many temples for Brahma.

LAKSHMI

Lakshmi is another goddess of the Tridevi. She represents beauty and **wealth**. Lakshmi is married to Vishnu.

Lakshmi is often shown holding lotus flowers. These symbolize that a search for wealth should be done for good reasons. Sometimes, she is shown sprinkling gold coins. This shows her love for her followers.

Lakshmi sometimes wears a pink sari. This stands for love and beauty.

Lakshmi is worshipped during Diwali. This is the Hindu festival of lights and usually lasts five days. During the festival, people pray to Lakshmi for good luck in the year ahead.

LIGHTING CANDLES FOR DIWALI

DAUGHTER OF THE SEA OF MILK

The story of Lakshmi's birth begins when the gods and demons wanted to create a potion. This potion would make whoever drank it live forever.

In the beginning, Earth's oceans were made of milk. To create the potion, the gods and demons stirred the ocean. Soon, figures began to rise from the milk.

One of those figures was Lakshmi. She rose up on a lotus flower, glowing with beauty. Lakshmi and Vishnu fell in love right away.

Lakshmi chose Vishnu to protect her. It is said the two are bound together by their love. Soon, Lakshmi gave birth to their son, Kama, who is the god of love.

PARVATI

Parvati is also a goddess in the Tridevi. Parvati is Shiva's wife and the goddess of love, marriage, and **fertility**.

Parvati and Shiva are both worshipped during a festival called Gangaur. This festival celebrates marriage. Women often pray to statues of Parvati and Shiva in their homes.

Parvati is often shown holding a trident. The three points of this kind of spear represent the things that make up a person. These are their passion, their good qualities, and their bad qualities.

Parvati is known by other names. These include Kali, the goddess of death, and Durga, the goddess of female warriors.

THE QUEST FOR SHIVA

Parvati had two sisters named Ragini and Kutila. All three of the sisters wanted to marry Shiva.

At the time, the universe was under threat from a terrible demon. Brahma said that Shiva's future wife would kill the demon. Parvati and her sisters trained to be ready for the fight.

All three sisters impressed the gods. Parvati's sisters were brought to Brahma. However, he said that neither of them would be able to kill the demon.

Brahma was most impressed by Parvati. Soon, Parvati married Shiva. When the day came for Parvati to fight the demon, she won! The world was safe again.

THE LEGENDS LIVE ON

Hinduism dates back more than 4,000 years. Today, it is the third largest religion in the world.

Hindu gods are worshipped and celebrated around the globe. The festivals and ceremonies for them will continue to bring people together for years to come.

GLOSSARY

ancestors people in a family who lived a long time ago

avatars different forms a god can turn into on Earth

BCE Before Common Era, the time before the year 1

cursed caused evil or bad things to happen

demons evil spirits or beings

divinity being a god or godlike

dusk the part of a day when it starts to get dark

fertility being able to have babies

legend a story from long ago

realm a different world

sari a traditional wrapped dress from India

wealth lots of something valuable, such as money

INDEX

READ MORE

Andrews, Elizabeth. *Hindu Mythology (Ancient Mythologies).* Minneapolis: Pop!, 2025.

Dickmann, Nancy. *Stars of Indian Mythology (Stars of Mythology).* New York: Gareth Stevens Publishing, 2026.

White, Kelly Anne. *Diwali and Other Hindu Celebrations (Holidays and Celebrations around the World).* San Diego, CA: Brightpoint Press, 2026.

LEARN MORE ONLINE

1. Go to **FactSurfer.com** or scan the QR code below.
2. Enter "**Hindu Gods**" into the search box.
3. Click on the cover of this book to see a list of websites.